Through the Darkness Into the Light

Memoirs of a Junkie

by

Catherine Bailey

To Kaelah

From Minister Bailey

470-623-3139

Love You xoxo 2019

Through the Darkness Into the Light
Memoirs of a Junkie

Printed in the United States of America through
Kindle Direct Independent Publishing Platform.
First Paperback Edition: November 2018

ISBN – 13: 9781729261743

Dedication

**To my family
who never gave up on me.**

Acknowledgements

Foremost, I would like to thank my family. I give a special shout-out to my children for having never given up on me (from oldest to youngest): My two daughters, Rahshanan Stevens-Washington and Tonique Dellaquila, and my son, AlTariq Bailey.

A shout-out to my two step-sons: Zakyrr Boyd and Ahmyrr Bailey. I raised them since they were six and three years old. God has also graced me with my other but not biological children: Wali Washington, Darius Dellaquila, Monique Bailey, and Teven Jones.

To my mother, Dorothy Stevens, my sister Elizabeth Stevens, and my other sister Patricia Stevens – both my elders – you saw something worthwhile in me even when I thought myself worthless. To all my sisters (Beatrice, Geneva, & Phyllis) who prayed for me, and to my brother Bobby, thank you. To my Spiritual Mother (Pastor Churn), you have been with me through this journey since I moved to Georgia. God had you keep me focused and to be my guardian angel. Pastor Churn has never let me down. She has been my prayer warrior. I thank God for her and appreciate beyond measure that she continues to help me conquer the challenges of life.

I also thank Bishop (Bishop Wilson) and my gorgeous First Lady (Wanda Wilson) of Solid Ground Ministries in Lithonia, GA. Both are a blessing in that I have learned much more about ministry from them. A funny side note: First Lady taught me how to dress like a "WOG" – a "Woman of God." I had it in me, but she helped to pull it out. Hence, I am the Woman of God who I am today. Additionally, I would like to thank my church family and friends. Also, a special shout-out to Pastor Roni whom God used to make me understand what it is to humble one's self.

I would like to thank God for Cathy Archambeault. Without her dedication and time doing the book cover and manuscript, none of this would have been possible. God does not make mistakes when He puts people in your life. She is my angel – I love you and thank you for all you did.

*

I have been through the fire, lost my way, stabbed in my back, discombobulated, wanted to kill myself, but however, I RISE!

Romans 8:28, "And we know that all things work for the good of those who love Christ Jesus that are called according to his purpose."

You would never know what you can accomplish when your foundation is built on the word of God. You can climb mountains and exorcise demons when your foundation is built on your faith in God. Some people who read this book may not agree with my belief and that is alright, but you can bet on this: "As for me and my household we will serve the Lord." (Joshua 24:15, New King James Version).

Psalm 69:1-3, "Save me, O God; for the waters are come in unto my soul. I sink in deep mire, where there is no standing: I am come into deep waters, were the flood overflow me. I am weary of my crying: my throat is dried: my eyes fail while I wait on my God."

Preface

This book depicts the journey of a downtrodden, desperate, and disillusioned junkie, sharing her pathway to discipleship with Christ. You might ask, "What is a junkie?" Metaphorically, a junkie is a person in bondage, locked up in solitary confinement, in a prison on a cell block without bars, no warden to curtail negative behavior, and no guards to keep you in check or facilitate and administer three-square meals and a cot. It is a person who loves and is addicted to more than one drug. A variety of drugs fill the menu and a junkie will partake until everything is finished. An addict can be addicted to many things: it may be drugs, food, shopping, or gossiping, but the appetite of a drug addict or junkie is insatiable. I think a disclaimer is in order: the ways in which I have defined addict or a junkie is based on my personal experiences and those of other addicts around me during this time. To this end, it may not encompass the behaviors of all addicts.

I decided to write this book because I wanted people to see that God can take what seems impossible and transform devil (drug) worship into restoration of life. I was a junkie when I arrived in

Georgia in 2005. Since that time, I have attended Seminary, experienced divorce, and graduated with a bachelor's and master's degree in Biblical Counseling. God gave me the miracle of recovery from an awful illness, allowed me to rediscover the person I once was, and led me to absorb the teachings of Jesus Christ.

As you read this book, my desire is for you all to bear witness to the hills, valleys, and mountains that God has navigated for me. I am still getting tested every day, but I have come to realize that going through trials and tribulations served to make me stronger. This book will acquaint you with those experiences and to illustrate that through the grace and mercy from God, my faith is ever-increasing.

Table of Contents

Through the Darkness into the LIGHT
Memoirs of a Junkie

Phase I:

Childhood (Age 5 to 20)

As I gaze back over my life and think about my parents and sibling relationships, I have much to be thankful for – even though my family was poor and oftentimes it was hard to make ends meet. One thing for sure, we were loved by our parents. I recall frequently moving from place to place, not having many clothes and sometimes being hungry, but we found a way to stay happy.

My mother was a homemaker and my father worked all the time. I was unaware, until I got my first real job at 18 years old, that employees were entitled to vacation time. It was then I realized that my father was always working because he had to feed eight children. Actually, I would describe the sibling clan as two sets of children. My oldest sister is older than I by twelve years. We were four older and four younger siblings growing up together with significant age disparities.

I had a good relationship with my parents although I remember fearing my father, along with

1

the rest of my siblings. My dad was very strong-willed and expected a lot from us. I have two brothers and five sisters. I am the seventh child. I had good relationships with all my siblings, but as mentioned before, the older ones didn't have much to say to the younger ones. I just remember them beating us up every chance they got while they laughed out loud.

We were definitely a dysfunctional family, and it was very difficult living in a house with so many personalities. I do believe there may be some hurt feelings or unfinished business with my family, but we are supportive of each other and have given our lives to God.

My mother will be eighty-eight in March of 2019, and God has truly shown her grace. My father went to be with the Lord in May of 1996. My parents had been married for forty-nine years when he passed. My oldest sister, Felicia, is sixty-nine years old. She has five children and many grandchildren. She attends Luther Rice University and will be graduating this year (2018) with a Bachelor's and Master's in Biblical counseling.

My oldest brother, James, passed on November 21, 2014, shortly after he retired from employment at the United States Postal Service on September 8. James also coached a youth softball team in Jersey City for a short period of time, which was something he really enjoyed. He didn't have any children, but he did leave behind a loving wife, Linda.

Geneva is sixty-six and is a graduate of New Jersey City University with her BA in counseling. She has three boys and five grandchildren.

Robert is the youngest of the older group of siblings and he is sixty-five years of age. He moved to Georgia a couple of years ago and fortunately receives veteran benefits for a service connected disability.

Now the second group of us consists of: Elizabeth, Patricia, Beatrice, and myself. Elizabeth is sixty-one and she adopted my sister Pat's six grandchildren. Pat is fifty-nine and works in a supervisory position for the Garden State Parkway Authority. She has retired as of this year, 2018. My youngest sister, Beatrice (fifty-six years old), retired early due to a work-related injury. My sister Beatrice also passed in February of 2018. I am the seventh child of the crew and I am fifty-eight.

I don't have anyone with which I need to mend or fix relationships. God has led me to apologize to all my siblings for the hurt and pain I caused them during my addictive hell. It is amazing that God has worked it out so that when they need prayer, they call on me. The scripture I give them is Matthew 11:28, "Come to me those who are heavy laden, and I shall give you rest."

I have so much peace knowing that through the Lord, all relationships that were torn and tattered due to my junkie lifestyle have been restored. I thank God that we are all still calling on the name of Jesus.

When I talk about my life as a child, I can remember being very poor more than anything else. My mother was a homemaker and my father … well, I would describe him as a "functional" alcoholic. One positive thing is that he was a dependable worker – a long distant bus driver. I remember when we moved to the housing projects, Curries Woods, my sister and I walked to Snyder High School with our friends. As we were walking, out of nowhere we heard a voice, "Hey, you two!" It was my father, drinking with the alcoholics (bums) in an empty lot.

Some of the kids teased me about my dad, which served as a catalyst for me getting into fights because I didn't know what else to do. However, my dad was a good dad to me and my sibling and I knew he loved all of his children no matter what he did or what we did. He also loved all of his grandchildren. He helped raise many of them because his children were unable to due to their addictions.

Earlier during my childhood, I can remember at the age of four I was angry because my mother had another child. So, one day I decided to put Drano in a tub with hot water and tried to submerge my baby sister – I guess with the thought of eliminating her.

My mother stopped me and, comparing that lashing to the others I had received, well let me say it is a wonder I am still here. I guess it would be fair to say I was a "bad seed." My mother told me stories about my behavioral pattern, and in hindsight, I must admit that I was a bad child.

I do recall punching my mother in the eye just because I was mad. It seems everything my mother told me *not* to do, I did. She told me not to ride on the back of the bike so quite naturally I disobeyed, and ended up getting my foot caught in the spikes with the resulting injury almost crippling me. I was rushed to the hospital and the doctor told my mother that if the injury had occurred an inch higher, I might have become crippled. I occasionally look at the scar and realize how thankful I am for the favor of God.

I can also remember living on Bright Street in Jersey City, New Jersey. We moved many times during my younger years. I remember my mother giving my sister a birthday party and my father's friend came over and got fresh with my sister. My mother almost stabbed my father to death for allowing that person to come to our home.

Maybe my violent gene was imported from her. I was quick to fight whenever anyone made fun of me. We were poor and some of the kids were cruel. I became angry and defiant at anyone I thought disrespected me because of my circumstances. I always fought a lot because I was teased about the way I looked, things I did not have, and of course, the drunk father. Drunk or not, he still was a great dad to us.

Actually, I believe I became addicted to fighting, as now I am going to focus on my time at Public

School Number Eight. The school was located on 96 Franklin Street in Jersey City. I resented being so poor that we used to eat bone soup, mustard sandwiches, ketchup sandwiches, and government cheese that never melted.

Picture that on a cold winter day, I had to wear my mother's stockings to keep warm on my way to school. I am like the shortest thing in the house and my mother is 5'9 inches. She put rubber bands around the top of the stockings to keep them from falling. Shortly after I arrived at school, this guy started chasing me. The reason I was running is because he liked me. I did not like him because he had "ring worms" and I was also afraid of him because he was a bully. As I was running, the stockings fell around my ankles and all I could hear were kids calling me "elephant legs." I started crying and ran home from school.

That is not the worst or most embarrassing thing in my young life. My 8th grade teacher, Mr. Pearson, was a very nice man. I was the only one in the class who wore skips. Skips were cheap sneakers. Everyone in this class, except for me, had shoes or Pro-Keds sneakers. If you had on Pro-Keds, you were considered to be the in-crowd.

Foolish me, I had not considered that only the boys were allowed to wear sneakers. I baby-sat for three weeks for five dollars and bought myself some hi-top Pro-Keds. (I had to hide the money from my mother because she liked to spend our money.) I bought the sneakers, tomboy that I was, and hid them in the empty apartment downstairs. Off I went to school with my new, bright white and red, name brand sneakers; I thought I was hot-stepping.

I went to class and the teacher called me outside and said "Catherine Stevens, you cannot wear sneakers in my classroom. Little girls are supposed to wear shoes!" I started crying and told him that my mother could not afford to buy me shoes and that I worked to get these sneakers so I wouldn't get teased at school. Later, that same teacher bought a bag of clothes and shoes for me. When he presented these gifts, all I could do was cry tears of joy.

I had been wearing under garments with holes in them. My sister wouldn't let me borrow hers so we didn't speak for two years. I endured getting teased and picked on for wearing not-so-gently used clothing and footwear. Often times, the clothes did not really fit me because of my small stature – which made matters even worse.

Fast-forward to high school. I found my niche playing basketball. The reason I started playing basketball was because of my friend, Lisa. She asked me plus five other girls whom we hung with to go play recreational basketball for Jersey City. We decided to do it, but here is the funny thing – we had no coach, so every time we went to play the other teams, we lost. It was alright; besides, we had nothing else to do. We played until the season was over and then they chose one girl from each team to play in the All- Star team. And guess who made the team? Yes! Me!

This was very important as it was Jersey City's first women's recreational team and I was chosen to represent my team. After the all-star game, we had a banquet for the teams that participated in the league. It was at night and I received two trophies (first time in my little life). The first trophy was for the team, even though we never won a game (laughing), and the second trophy was for winning the all-star game.

This put me on the road to play basketball for Snyder High School. I made the team as a point guard. The best thing about being a member of the team was we got brand new white, high-top Converse shoes plus white socks with orange and black – the Snyder High School colors.

When you start playing sports in school, you get unwanted attention from boys/girls that you do not need. While I was becoming popular for playing basketball, this boy named Les heard about me and wanted to get to know me. He introduced himself to me and I, unaware of his intentions, told him my name. Then the nonsense started. I was already mad because Reggie had broken up with me and so I decided, okay, let me talk to Les. That was a BIG MISTAKE!

One day at school, Les invited me to his house. Being naïve, I played hooky from school (skipping class) to meet Les at his house. That was when he tried to rape me – at fourteen years old. This was a horrific time for me. I was already hurting from the break-up from Reggie, and when you try to get even with someone, trust me – it hurts you even more.

 Since I would not comply with his demand, he started to rip my clothes off and, of course, I gave a fight. He almost succeeded, but I had a fight in me and I cried as I fought for my virginity. I know I gave a good fight because he yelled, "Get the [explicative] out, you [explicative]!" Yes!

I was crying when he threw me out of his house. I left, looking and peeking so nobody could see me. I was ashamed of myself; I felt disrespected, scared, and had an uncanny feeling.

Mind you, he lives right across the street from Snyder High School where we both attended. Walking down the street on Bergen Avenue, with tears in my eyes, Howard saw me and he asked me,

"Cat, what's wrong with you?" Howard walked me home, and later after calming down, I braided his hair which I often did. It was then that I shared what happened earlier – what Les had done to me. Howard got this strange look on his face and said for me not to worry. I finished his hair and he looked at me and said, "Les will never put his hands on you again!" Howard's eyes were big and he had this look that spooked me, but I never knew that Howard was going to beat up Les.

Later, he kicked Les' behind and told him not to ever touch me again! I found out that Les got a good old fashioned butt-whooping. That was the first time anyone, other than my siblings, fought for me. Howard came to my house afterward and informed me of what he had done. I hugged him with tears in my eyes and he said, "Cat, I will always be here for you!" He was right because still, to this day, Howard still loves me the same way he did back in the day. We still keep in contact with each other.

Before we moved to Bergen Avenue, it was a plethora of places we had moved. I will take you down the several places we lived that I can remember. I remember moving from Bright Street to Grand Street, from Grand Avenue to Bergen Avenue and into a house. From Bergen Avenue, we moved to an apartment in the basement, and after that we moved to Stevens Avenue. Then we moved to Dwight Street, and the last and final destination was Curries Woods Project until I graduated from Snyder High, as did all three of the younger sisters except for Pat. She moved out at the age of eighteen right after graduation because she was pregnant. She moved in with the father of her child.

I was a mischievous child in high school. I fought a lot and was always arguing with my teachers. I hated school. I can remember fighting one particular time with a girl because my friend, Lisa, convinced me that she was "kicking my back in" (that is talking bad about you). I told Lisa that I was going to (explicative) her up! (Yes, my mouth was filthy.) Well, of course Lisa did not believe me. (Lisa just wanted to see if I could fight.) Therefore, I said, "I tell you what. If I kick her behind, you have to pay my way to Saint Peter's Party!" Oh, those parties back in my day were a big deal and the place to be!

Lisa said, "You're not going fight Cynthia."

I said back, "You've got the money for the party?"

Lisa answered, "I got you; I just don't think you're going to do it."

I said, "Why not?"

Lisa answered, "Because you don't fight ... you're the good one!"

I laughed to myself, and then said, "See, don't let my height and because I don't say much fool you!"

"Alright, I got you." Lisa grinned teasingly. "Let's go see where she's going to be in the auditorium."

"Lisa! Don't play with my money! You know I like going to those parties and my mother doesn't have the money."

"I got you," Lisa teased. "You're just scared!"

Lisa and I walked into the auditorium. Cynthia was there, talking smack. Now mind you, I'm not scared, but my adrenaline is pumping because this girl is 5'11" and I'm 4'11" tall! I walked up to her and she said to me: "What do you want (expletive)?" Before she finished saying the word "B-I-T-C ..," I punched her in face – BOOM! I had to jump up because I was so short. When I punched her, she fell back into the chairs and then I jumped on her and commenced to whooping her butt.

Yes, I wanted to go to that party. At this point, I was just tired of people talking about me, my clothes, my house, my sisters – it all had become a little too much. As I was beating her up, everything I was going through went into her beating. Unfortunately, she caught all of my frustrations. I beat that girl so bad she started screaming, "GET HER OFF OF ME!" The security guards came and literally pulled me off of her and escorted me to the principal's office. Her face was bruised, she had busted lip, and a black eye.

Now, my mother had to come and pick me up. My mother always said, "If I come to school for you, you had better tell me the truth." Now I *am* scared – my mother was not joking.

I did not know Cynthia had told the principal that she was jumped by me and five other girls. My mother got to the school and asked me, "What happened?" I told her that Cynthia and I had a fight because she kept talking about me. Next, the principal called my mother into his office with me and informed her that she had to take me down to the Police station.

My mom asked, "Why do I have to take her to the Police station?"

The Principal answered, "Cynthia said your daughter and five girls jumped her."

"She's lying!" My mom exclaimed. "My daughter doesn't need help kicking a girl's behind, especially if the girl keeps bothering her!"

"You have to go to tell your daughter's side to the police," the principal said.

"Will do!" my mom said.

Now we are at the Police station. Understand, the only person, besides my father, I was scared of was my mother, but as long as you told her the truth, she will fight the battle to the end. My father drove my mother and me (funny, my dad happened to be home at this time although he was never home). My mother grabbed my hand tightly and again she looked at me and said, "You better be telling the truth!"

I said, "Mom, I did not jump her. I fought her so she would stop talking about me." We entered the Precinct and a cop was standing behind the counter. I heard the officer ask, "Is Cathy here?"

My mother said, "Yes, she is my daughter."

Then the cop said, "Where is she?" (I was so short that he couldn't see me.)

My mother said softly, "She's right here."

He looked over the counter and started laughing, "Ma'am, what happened?"

My mother explained, "My daughter told me this girl was bothering her and she beat her up!"

The police officer asked, "This little thing right here beat that tall girl up all by herself?"

"Yes," my mom answered. "Why'd you ask that? Is that unbelievable?"

"The girl, Cynthia, made a report that your daughter and five other girls jumped her," the officer said. "No way this tiny little girl beat her up that bad!"

"Officer, my daughter fought her and beat her up by herself," my mom defended me. "She does not need any help from her friends. The other girl is lying. Ask my daughter and the witnesses."

The officer asked me, "What happened?" I explained to him what had happened and he started laughing again. I could see his belly going up and down and I smirked. "This is funny. I don't know how this little thing right here beat the other girl up so badly. You know what? Take her home!" The officer was still laughing when we left.

Attending school was not something I wanted to do. I hated school! No one would enjoy being somewhere and be teased all the time, so my basketball gave me peace. Going to parties was also one of the things I liked about growing up. The rest you can have. I was not a good student, but I went because I had to.

*

Now, this is really important. One winter, when we lived on Bergen Avenue (a short distance from Snyder High School) our gas and electricity were turned off. There were icicles on the windows and the students passing by referred to our home as the "Monster house." We were evicted from that "Monster house" and subsequently moved to several locations before settling in the Curries Woods Housing Projects in Jersey City.

As I referenced earlier, we endured years of moving from place to place. Then, we unexpectedly moved to my sister's apartment with her husband and children! Yup, you guessed it, but even if you didn't, when we moved to Curries Woods Project, my sister already had a husband and four children. Now it was really rough because my father was not around, and to ask me where he was, I would tell you, "your guess is as good as mine." Yeah! PAPA WAS A ROLLING STONE! But, he was still my dad and I loved him and he did what he knew to do.

This was not good for the family and definitely bad for me. While staying there, I went to sleep one night and I felt a hand on me. I jumped up and it was my sister's husband touching me. Now I'm scared because we don't have anywhere to go – my father was not around and my mother was not working. I did not want to live on the street. I was scared to tell my mom what happened, so I told my

15

sister, Poochie. My sister and I hatched a plan. She told me that she would stay up and pretend she was sleeping. I would pretend to be sleeping as well. My sister's husband came into the living room again. As he was about to touch me, my sister jumped out of the closet and screamed, "Mom! Sam is in here trying to touch Cathy!" (We did not know what molesting was). My mother grabbed a knife and threatened that if he ever touched me or any of her girls again, she would kill him.

Sam worked for the Housing Authority and that is how we were able to move to 71 Merritt Street in Curries Woods. He didn't help us because he wanted to or because he had a good heart. He helped to make that happen because he did not want to get killed by my mother. So, since he worked for the Projects, he had, as we call, "Clout!" We moved to 71 Merritt Street and my father moved in after Poochie, Beatty, my mother, and I moved the furniture we had from 9 Heckman Drive in Curries Woods to 71 Merritt Street.

Oh, yeah, my father moved back in. I go back to this part and again, if it was not for God's grace and mercy, I probably would not be here writing this book. There is but so much you can take and I am glad God watched over me once again.

My friend, Lisa, and I were best friends during this time. We were friends since the eighth grade and now Lisa liked a young boy named Chris. Lisa and I were always going to the Projects because that is where Chris lived. Lisa liked getting in trouble and so did I, as you already know. Lisa lived right down the street from me when I lived on Bergen Avenue and unfortunately, we had to move, but Lisa would come to Dwight (yeah, I forgot, after Stevens Avenue, it was Dwight Street).

Lisa came one day and said (at this time I was fifteen years old), "Shorty (that was my nickname), do you want to walk with me to Chris' house?"

"Where does he live?" I asked.

"The Projects."

"Which one?" I asked. (There were several housing projects in Jersey City.)

"Shorty, it's not that bad," Lisa reassured me. (She was never scared because she was from New York.)

"Okay," I agreed.

I went and changed out of my clothes into something more eye-catching. I threw on my good jumpsuit and it fit like a glove! You couldn't tell me anything; it was tight, small waistline, and I had a big butt and you know I had that "walk" too. So, I went with Lisa and when we decided to leave I heard a voice say, "Excuse me, what's your name?"

Now, I'm in the 11th grade and I turned around and said, "Who are you talking to?"

The young boy said, "You!"

(I'm smiling at this time but scared at the same time.) I stopped to acknowledge him and he asked my name again. I gave him my name and he said, "Damn! You look good in that jumpsuit! Can I get a number?"

I said, "No!" What he did not know was that I did not have a number to give him. The mysterious guy's name was Russell (my oldest daughter's father). I told him that if he wanted to talk to me then he would have to find me. This is how I met Russell. He said he was going to find me because he really liked me.

I lived on what we called "The Hill" on Dwight Street. One day, I was sitting on the porch and Russell rode by. He said, "Ah ha! I found you! I told you I was going to find you." He asked me what I was doing and I told him I was trying to get something to eat for my sister and me. He said he was broke, so I told him to get to stepping because there was nothing he could do for me.

Later that night, I saw my mother's friend, Ms. Lois, leaving the house with her friend. I heard her tell her two daughters to stay in the house, but they never listened. So, I squatted. I knew they were going to leave because they were bad, and as expected, they made their exit. When they left, I told my sister Beatty, "Let's go and get something to eat."

"Where're we going? You're always up to something!"

I responded, "Be quiet and follow me and don't tell momma because we will get our behinds beat!" We went in Mrs. Lois's house and, luckily for us, she had made some beef stew with big chunks of beef in it. We ate all the stew and ravaged through the house for anything else that we could have used.

That night we were full but the next night we were hungry again. My childhood days were often painful, many sleepless nights, hunger pains, name-calling, and missing our father a lot. Watching the tearful eyes of my mother was heartbreaking. I intentionally did not mention holidays because they were the most excruciating! Fathom this: a child getting teased because they had to wear holey clothes, wear skips, suffer abuse, endure name-calling, fighting all the time, instability, an alcoholic father, and just trying to survive. Scholarships were offered, but why take them when you didn't have the money to go? Everything started spiraling out of control. Farewell my childhood and young adulthood; I never have to see you again.

Children today have it too easy. They are always complaining and could never have gone through what we went through as children and young adults. Children, young adults, tweens, or whatever this generation calls themselves today, should go after their dreams, listen to their parents, and cement their foundation on the promises of God. I was lost but I survived – can you? I wanted to be loved but didn't know how to give love. I fell in love with Russell Posey – at least so I thought. Russell and I had our first child, a daughter, when I was 20 years old. I finally had someone to love me unconditionally.

We planned her. After I had our daughter, Rahshanan, he left me for another woman. Shortly thereafter, I tried to kill myself. But God saved me again! I had my beautiful daughter out of this deal and she loved me no matter what I did. But, I didn't know how to be a mother; the only thing I knew was pain.

My dear friends, do not think that if you have a baby then you are going to keep a man. You had better hold onto God because He said in His Word, "Do not trust in man because he will always disappoint you. Trust in God!" Some things just don't seem natural to me now that I am 58 years old. I am trying to give the Teens, Tweens (so they call them today), young adults, and adults, insight. Make right choices, go to school, and most importantly, don't be a fool!

From Proverbs 3:5-6 "Lean not unto your own understanding. Trust in God and He will order your steps!" Always build your foundation on God and He will order your steps and make sure the grace of God will never take you where the will of God is not. It is important for the person reading this to understand that no one is exempt from this wicked world.

Be careful of the choices you make and know that if your foundation is not built around God, you are certainly doomed! If you do not believe in God now, maybe by the time you finish reading this book, you will look at the people you hang with, the decisions you make, and more importantly remember: God shows grace on the Righteous and Unrighteous.

I sit here and realize, "What if I had done it a different way? What if I had accepted those scholarships for basketball? What if I never tried to kill myself at sixteen, nineteen, etc.? Even if I could of, would of, or should of, I did not, and this is my Memoirs. I hope and pray that you think before you take a wrong turn.

Phase 2:

The Beginning of the Drug and Dark Era

I never thought a person could go through so much by becoming a victim of an environment of their own creation. I was that person and if you were to ask me if I liked what I did, I would have to say, "NO!" But if you ask me if I regret what I did, I would have to say, "NO!" I guess you are wondering, "What is this woman talking about?"

BOOM! Here I am, twenty years old and hanging out with a young woman I knew since High School. She had one child and was doing her own thing: living in her own apartment, getting high, and entertaining as many men who met her fancy.

I had transitioned from living in a house to an apartment to a housing project. What a big difference and adjustment that was for me. I started hanging out with the wrong crowd and that was when my horror began. I will take you down a dark road that no one should ever travel. Let me start by saying that living a life filled with drugs, hitmen, police, backstabbers, snitches, and the ungodly, leads to death here on earth.

My problem was drugs. I call them the Scarecrow, Tin man, and the Lion. That was my nickname for my drugs. The Scarecrow was my heroine, the Tin man was my cocaine, and the Lion was my pills and Methadone. As a junkie, I was always looking for the Oz – the drug dealer. A junkie will get his/her fix – Oz saw me every day. I can truly say one thing about using drugs: the Oz will see you. It could be raining, snowing, sleeting, hurricane, tornado, tsunami, or mud-slide, but I promise you, a junkie will go get that fix. I used for over twenty years, and for some reason, God saw something in me and saved me.

This life took me down to the lowest part of the earth that I never thought I would ever experience. This was during the years from 1980-1989 that got me caught up with craziness. Now, I told you my daughter's father left me for another woman, but when he heard I was on drugs, he returned into my life and that is when I really started spiraling out of control. However, by the time Russel came back in my life, I had already been introduced to Cocaine, pills, and heroine. He was disappointed with me, but he had to take some responsibility for why I chose to venture off into the dark world.

Here I am, hanging out with my girlfriend and was introduced to cocaine. Baby, when I first sniffed the white power named cocaine, I was confused because I did not feel high and everybody around me was feeling good. I need to inform you that zebras and codeine were pills you took together to get high. I took those three times and did not get high, but the fourth time I took them it knocked me off my feet. I was feeling so good … like I was in another body. Those were the street names for these pills. You took both to simulate the effect of dope and cocaine. It made you nod and then picked you up. It was a good high and we would go to Newark, New Jersey, to buy them because it was cheaper to go to Newark then to buy them off the streets in Jersey City. Not only did we take those pills, we took: footballs (downers), Quaaludes (downers), and purple haze (uppers). But, for the most part, we took anything that would make us high.

I then was introduced to this older gentleman who hung out at the bar we went to. Of course, my friend who I went with had a hidden agenda. I found that out later, after I was date-raped by this man, that she had promised him that I would have sex with him for cocaine and a drink. AIN'T THAT SOME MESS! I did not know until he took out a load of cocaine, took me to a nice bar, and asked me, "Do you want to go to the hotel to talk?"

Being ignorant and high, I said, "Alright. Do I have to do anything?"

He told me, "No."

Not in my right mind, I said, "Cool." I was thinking to myself that I would get cocaine, free drinks, and I could rest.

Well, it did not go that way. My naiveté got me attacked. He started trying to pull off my clothes (mind you I am about 100 pounds soaking wet and 19 years old before I had my daughter.) I started screaming and he put his hands over my mouth. I yelled, "STOP! PLEASE! PLEASE STOP!"

He looked at my face and saw the tears running down my cheeks and he said, "I am sorry. She told me that if I provide you with drugs and a drink, you would have sex with me."

I said that I was not like what she described me to be, and he realized that I had been set up. I cried and cried because I was disappointed with myself for being so stupid. You would think that I learned from that, right? NO! I still hung out with the very same person who set me up. Why? I now had a taste for that life – I was in too deep! I was not working and the men would supply whatever drugs I needed.

Eating lobster and drinking Pipers, Don Perrier, or Moet at the bar – you were a big deal! I was stupid, because the guy that date- raped me sent me a box of Moet, two silk dresses, a bottle of Jontu Perfume, and apologized for his actions. Yes, I was stupid, but I liked what I was doing. Here I am, now lost in a world that I thought I knew.

To be honest, I never understood how a human being who has used drugs could introduce another human being to that life. Understand, "THEY NEVER TELL YOU THE DOWNFALLS, THE SICKNESS, AND WHAT YOU HAVE TO DO TO GET THAT DRUG!" At the end of the day, I could have said "no," but unfortunately as the saying goes, "You are a product of your environment!" My environment was full drugs, drug addicts, drug dealers, poverty, dilapidated infrastructure, high crime, failing schools, single parent homes, and a government that couldn't care less until it was voting time. All of this is a recipe for disaster and is NOT conducive to a productive life for anyone.

Meanwhile, now I am getting high, Russell is in my life, and we moved to Three Heckman Dr. in Curries Wood Projects. Here I am selling drugs, getting high, and not taking care of my first child. She was taken from me by my nephew who said to me, "When you get your life together, come get your daughter!" In hindsight, that turned out to be the best thing I could have done for my child. Mind you, I'm selling drugs and buying clothes from the booster (people who steal clothes from the store). You cannot tell me anything; I think I am good but my habit is getting worse.

The darker era is when P-Funk came out. You may ask, "What is 'P-Funk'?" It is heroine that is so potent you can die from it. They take heroine that can take a seven cut and put a three cut on it. You get so high it lasts until the next day. Many of my friends had died from shooting up P-Funk. The names they put on the packages of heroine were names like: Black Eagle, Poison, Red Devil, Blue Sky, some would have just a symbol on it, and many other names, but it made you so high.

I moved up from pills (any kind if I got high) to cocaine, but now I'm using all three. I'm selling drugs and "speed balling" (mixing heroine with cocaine), and taking pills. I think I "got it going on" while not acknowledging that my daughter is no longer with me, and my mother, my father, and my sister Liz, were making sure she had all that she needed. Here's how my life becomes painful.

Chronicles of Near Death

Imagine working in a "shooting gallery," having a sawed-off shot gun in your face, nine-millimeter gun to your head, sodomized, beat with a pistol for an hour, and date-raped – all for the love of drugs. Calling on Jesus was the best thing I could have done.

I was using and selling drugs, and Russell decided for us to work in the shooting gallery. What is a shooting gallery? It is a place where many addicts/junkies go to shoot up drugs. Now, I am hustling, buying stolen clothes, and watching out for the hit men and snitches all at the same time. I had to be alert and I learned the hard way why Russell always told me, "Be careful when you are bringing the package to the shooting gallery!"

The shooting gallery was one of the places I experienced two of the most horrific tragedies in my life. Russell and I were selling drugs at the shooting gallery. We sold the packages we had brought with us, so I had to go and get another package from where I was living. Now, I informed everybody in the house (my mother's house on the 4th floor residing at 71 Merritt St. In Curries Woods

Projects) not to tell anybody were Russell and I were. However, a man asked my sister where we were and she had the nerve to tell them we were on the fifth floor at the shooting gallery, selling drugs.

I didn't know that when I went downstairs to get some packages to sell, two hitmen were hiding. As soon as I knocked on the door of the shooting gallery, they grabbed me. When they grabbed me, they put a sawed-off shot-gun in my face and said, "Knock on the door and if Russell doesn't answer, I'll blow your head off!" Mind you, the gun is in my face. I am shaking and ready to faint. I started knocking on the door and of course Russell came to the door with the chain lock on and said, "Cat?"

I responded, "Yes!"

Russell opened the door and saw that they had a gun in my face! The hitman grabbed me by my neck tighter and said, "Look man, I am going to count to three. If you don't open the door, I'm going to blow your girl's brains out!"

The hit man started to count, "one ... two ..." and he pulled the trigger. He yelled, "DAMN! This never happened before!" The gun jammed! When Russell heard him trying to shoot it again, he opened the door. They robbed everybody in the house and took all of the drugs. Now, I am hyperventilating, shaking, and scared as I don't know what! I was sick for a month. Then, I was finally ready to go back to being STUPID!

While inside the bathroom of the shooting gallery, I watched a woman shoot dope in a vein in her neck. I was like, "What the hell is this?" Suddenly, the shooting gallery got hit again! I was trying to hide behind the shower curtain and, of course, they found me and ordered me to go get the drugs! They put a 9MM gun to my head and said if I didn't hurry, they would come to where I lived.

I went and got the drugs, but I had to do a bag of P-Funk (both times) to calm me down. After that stick-up (robbery), I could not face another. So, Russell and I started selling out of my mother's house until we moved in with my girlfriend. Let me tell you something – yes, you who are reading this book, – do me a favor: if someone, somebody, anyone or anybody (especially your friends) tries to introduce drugs into your life, please say "NO!"

My life did not get any better after that. Russell was sleeping with anybody in a skirt, dress, or pants. At this point, we were living with my friend. One day, her man came by the house and I knocked on the door because I had gone across the hall to see my mother. When I entered, my friend and her man said, "Come here, try this!" I asked them what it was and they said it was called "free-basing."

I asked if it were that stuff that the comedian was set on fire by doing, and they answered, "Yes!" Now, you are wondering, if I knew that this was going to get me addicted, then why did I go and do it? As you read earlier, I did everything I thought was cool. I was trying to fill a void. Although I had a large family, I often felt alone and awkward.

Okay, back to the story. So, I take a pull. It was a bottle that was round and had a little hole on one side and a stem about 5 inches long that you pull through. White smoke fills the stem and water is at the bottom of the glass bottle.

They offered for me to come and take a pull. Like a fool, I did and BOY! I liked it a lot! After I started smoking cocaine, it takes you to a place you do not want to go. I felt good. I had just done a bag of P-Funk and then took a pull of that cocaine. I was hooked! I was smoking cocaine, doing heroine, and still doing smack (also heroine but not as strong as P-Funk). Now, every day we are smoking, but Russell did not like free-basing, so I started tapping the bags of dope and cocaine just to buy more cocaine.

I became my biggest customer and did not know how to stop. One day, one of our customers came to buy two twenty bags of dope and four nickel (they were in aluminum foil) bags of cocaine. You could always tell the people who shot drugs and people who smoked and people who just sniff. We even knew the people who put the cocaine in their weed. It was crazy, scary, and sad.

I got mad at Russell because he was sticking around with whom I thought was my friend, so one day I convinced Russell to take a hit of cocaine. I wanted to take revenge on him for always cheating on me and messing around with one of my associates. I convinced him to try freebasing and got him hooked. Now once he got hooked, things turned for the worse. He took this girl out and my sister caught them going into my so-called friend's house right next door to my mother.

Well, you know my sister called me and said, "Cathy get over here now!"

I responded by asking, "Why?" I was already mad because Russell did not bring my drugs yet and I was getting sick. I really didn't want to hear my sister call and tell me that Russell, Calvin, Denise, and Sheryl were going into Denise's house – disrespecting me. Here I am, dope-sick waiting for Russell to bring my drugs so I can feel better, and he is sneaking into Denise's house with Sheryl.

Well, my sister said, "Get your butt over here! I'm tired of them pretending to be your friends while they are having sex with your man!"

It made me sick and frustrated, because I trusted these two young ladies and they were doing me dirty. So, I got myself together, went over to my mother's house, and caught them going into Denise's house. I burst into the house and grabbed Sheryl. I beat the mess out of her. I took her by her braids and her butt and was banging her head into the wall and ripping out her braids. When I got finished whooping her, I heard my sister tell my other sister to whoop Denise's butt too, because she had the nerve to bring that girl into the house with Russell to cheat on Cathy. Honey, I tell you that my sister went and punched Denise out of her shoes.

I stopped her and said, "This is my fight!" I grabbed Denise and started fighting her too. I beat the living daylights out of her – from East to West and from North to South. I was just so hurt by them. I told them both that if I caught them on 3 Heckman side, I was going to beat them up on sight, every time. It was sad because this was not the only time I had to fight because of Russell.

Russell was dealing with a girl who used to pick on me every time she saw me, and she always had her friend with her. I would always tell my mother about this girl who didn't like me because I was Russell's girlfriend. One day, when I was going to visit Russell, she and her friend got on the same elevator with me. They kept calling me names. A lady said to them, "Leave her alone because one day she is going to beat the both of you."

She didn't lie! One day, I was standing in front of 7 Heckman Dr. and who walked up to the building while I am talking to my gentleman friend? You guessed it – it was that same girl. She was with her male friend and they went upstairs. When she came back down, she had grease on her face and sneakers on. Back in the day, those were fighting actions. I said to my friend, "She is trying to hint that she wants to fight me."

My friend said, "Cat, PLEASE don't fight her, you'll hurt that girl!"

I told my friend that this girl had been picking on me for almost a year and now she just came downstairs with grease on her face, sneakers on, and her hair combed down. I said that I would be right back. I never forget that day because Russell and I had broken up again and I was feeling down. I just wanted to kill somebody that day. Well, I ran home, changed from my red dress to a pair of pants and a blouse, put grease on my face and told my mother that I was going to fight that girl that kept picking with me.

I ran out the door and when I got over to 7 Heckman, my sisters were right behind me. Well, she was sitting on the car and I said, "What you want to do?"

Her response was, "Whatever!"

My sister said, "Cat, we didn't come here to hear you ask questions! Do what you came to do!" The boy with the girl stepped up and my sister pulled a gun out – it was a BB gun but he didn't know that. My sister yelled, "STEP BACK! Or I will blow your head off!"

He stepped back, and my sister said, "Now kick her behind!" The girl threw a punch but I ducked and then punched her – BAM!! She fell back on the car and I grabbed her from her head and butt and picked her up and dropped her onto the ground – BOOM!! The building shook and the people looked out their windows. I was beating this girl like she stole something from me. I jumped on her back, head, face, and when I went to jump on her again, my sister grabbed me in the air and said, "Cat! That's enough, you're going to kill her."

Russell appeared from somewhere and ran over to me. My sister snarled, "Step back, you low life

or pick her up from the airport. I remember when I was in second grade, my mom was supposed to buy me a Halloween costume for a school party. We hadn't seen her in a while, and on the morning of the party we thought she wasn't coming with the costume, so my grandmother threw a sheet on me and I was a ghost. Then right before I was about to leave, my mom popped up with a witch costume and a big ole white teddy bear. I swear it was bigger than I was! I loved and cherished that bear. So, I got dressed in my new costume and she painted my face. It was a good day. She came through.

After that, events became blurry for me. I know my mom said that she and I went to visit Russell in Texas when I was about six years old. All the while, I was still living with my grandparents, and my parents were still drug addicts. My mother got clean from drugs by the time I was nine years old – that was in 1989. She met a new guy who later became my step-father, Greg Bailey. He had two boys of his own and an ex-wife. He was a regional manager for McDonald's, right around the corner from the projects. We were introduced. At that time, my mother was working for the Garden State Parkway in New Jersey which was a big deal because it paid well and afforded her benefits. It changed her life.

I lived with my mother and her then boyfriend, Greg, for a short while in Duncan Projects. I was in the eighth grade. She found out she was pregnant with my sister, Tonique. She and Greg got married in grandiose fashion. Such a big wedding cost a lot of money, and she went into debt paying for it. I remember that time of my life clearly because I was angry that she didn't have the money to take me school shopping for my first year in high school. I flunked the first semester on purpose as sort of a rebellion. But it backfired because I was punished and still didn't get school clothes until I passed the next semester.

Then, my sister was born in January of 1993. She was my step-father's first biological girl so he was elated. We all were still living in Duncan projects until I moved back in with my grandparents shortly after she was born. I completed my freshman year. They then moved to an apartment in East Orange, New Jersey. They were moving on up. My mother always tried to be active in my life so, when they moved, I went to live with them too. I transferred to Clifford J. Scott in East Orange and started my sophomore year there. I had my own room for the first time. She was working steadily and taking care of the family. Life was good.

I got robbed on my way to school one morning, and then two more times in Newark, NJ, and in East Orange. We all thought it was best that I move back in with my grandparents. In 1995, my mother got pregnant again with her baby boy, AlTariq, who was born in 1996. Shortly thereafter, everything started spiraling out of control again.

I was now out of high school and enrolled in college. I was living my new adult life. We got a call from Greg, my step-father, asking my grandmother to come over to the house because he and my mother had gotten into a fight. I happened to be there at my grandmother's and decided to go with her because I hadn't seen them in a while.

When we get there, things just didn't seem right. My mother had been losing a lot of weight and Greg looked disheveled. We knew something was wrong. Greg began to tell us that my mother had relapsed and was stealing his money for drugs. Prior to this, my mother was on workmen's compensation because she had gotten robbed while on the job.

Anyway, back to the revelation that she had relapsed. I was heartbroken and in disbelief. That news rocked my world! I went back home wondering what the hell had happened, what had I missed, and why hadn't I seen the signs. Later in life, I realized that this relapse was most damaging to me because I was in the process of transitioning from a young lady into a woman and I needed my mother to teach me life lessons that others could not. For example, I needed her to teach me about men, about being a mother, and most importantly about the streets. Consequently, I've made many mistakes while dealing with men and in general life that probably could have been avoided had I gotten some guidance.

Anyway, over the course of the years, my sister and brother were the ones who suffered the most because they lived with them while they were addicts. There were times when they had to live with my aunt and grandmother, and other times they had to live with me. But as the old saying goes, "It takes a village to raise a child!" We all helped in one way or another. I think the younger kids had it the worst because they witnessed it as opposed to being left with a family member and therefore not having to see it first-hand.

In hindsight, I have learned that this was the path God had in store for me. I didn't do too badly. In 2005, my mother and step-father decided to get clean and went into recovery. They relocated to Georgia in 2005 with my sister and brother. By this time, I had met my now husband and had another child following shortly thereafter. This was a whole new chapter in our lives. We were starting over. My mom and step-dad purchased their first home in Lithonia. We came down and stayed with them for a while and then moved out on our own. We had a few set-backs and had to move back in with them twice. Ultimately, we did get our lives together.

Although our lives weren't peaches and cream, I would not change it for the world. I had a wonderful childhood despite not having both parents. What I do regret is not being able to build that mother-daughter bond with her earlier than we did. Now I have six living children and one who passed away in 2015 and another one on the way. I have been with my husband for 15 years. I can attribute that to my parents who were absent because I vowed to never leave my children. I know from experience how damaging that can be and the toll it takes on them.

Now, my mother has been clean for thirteen years and counting. She's accomplished a lot of post-addiction work and we are proud of her. She is not perfect, neither are any of us, but she tries. She's managed to acquire her bachelor's and master's degree, is a homeowner, a grandmother, and a woman of God. She has become a minister and a Biblical counselor. We are proud of her!

Summarizing My Life Through Biblical Characters:

When you are in this life, you never know what you are going to do to get that next hit, next fix, or that high after you first took a hit off that glass stem. You are a "wolf in sheep's clothing" and you go through life chasing a high you will never get again. Know that first hit of the pipe is the best and you will go on to try to get that feeling again, but you NEVER DO!!!!

Rahab: The Prostitute
Jacob: The Deceiver
Aaron: The Idolatry
David: The Adulterer
Gideon: Afraid

The names above fit perfect with my life in the drug and dark era. Rahab was a prostitute, but she did this to take care of her family. On the other hand, I was Rahab so to not wake up sick. Rahab knew important people and had status. She knew the King and I knew the people who had the best drugs.

42

Now Jacob was a big deceiver who asked his brother to sell his birthright for a bowl of soup … and his brother did. I was Jacob because I could deceive anybody to get me the drugs I needed. I didn't care if you were married, had a boyfriend, or were engaged. Cathy got what she wanted when she needed it the most.

Aaron was an idolater who worshiped the golden calf. Unlike Aaron, I worshipped my drugs instead of a golden image. It was as if I did not get my heroine or have my glass stem, then I could not get out of the bed. I would shake, have diarrhea, and could not eat or sleep. Restless leg syndrome has nothing on the cramps from heroin addiction.

David not only was a murder but was also an adulterer. Well, I was too. I would go to a woman's house and tell them in advance that if you try to jerk me, I will take your man. Married or not, at that time I did not give a DARN!! I just wanted my drugs and to get high. That was the attitude I had to have, or I would have been lost in that world.

Gideon was afraid because every time he planted seeds and they grew, the Midianites would terrorized the Israelites and take all that they had planted. So, God used Gideon to fight against the Midianites so they could eat. I also was Gideon because I was afraid that when I got high with men, if I ran out after smoking their cocaine and sniffing their dope, they would hurt me. So, I would always find a way to beat them and prayed they did not run up on me. So, I was afraid and had to keep looking over my back to not get beat down.

Nearly Beaten to Death

Now, Russell and I had ended our relationship. He moved to Texas because there was a "hit" out on his head as well as my head. My turn came but, when the guy pushed in my door and realized I used to hang out with his brother and him, he told me to stay in the house. He told me that Big Dog put a hit out on Russell and me because Russell owed him money. Big Dog was the big drug dealer in Curries Woods, and he had a lot of hustlers working for him. He was the type of man who smoked "Angel Dust Weed" and would get so high that he would always chew bubblicious gum to bring him down. A lot of people were scared of him … and who could blame them? Big Dog was a big man and was known for getting people killed and setting them up. However, Big Dog eventually lost his life in a "New York execution" style.

I stayed in the house for about two weeks and Russell moved to Texas. Russell remained in Texas until this day! I continued to use drugs and my mother, father, and sister raised my child Rahshanan. After all I went through with Russell, I found another crazy guy named Bruce. I knew him from high school. I was staying with my sister, Pat, and met him. At that time, I was working at Bank of America, but I got fired for what was described as "dressing too provocatively."

Before being fired, I started going downstairs and hanging out with Bruce and his woman and getting them high every time I got paid. I told her that when she got her welfare check, she needed to come and see about me. Well, she thought I was playing, so her man came upstairs and said, "Dee got her money but told me not to get you because she is not getting you high."

I got up and put on my sexy skirt and my high heeled shoes. Then I went downstairs and said, "I told you that when you get paid I want my portion of drugs and you refused to invite me! So, I'm taking what you love!" And I did … it was her man!

We started dating and boy, what a colossal mistake! He became mean and overbearing. I couldn't go anywhere. He actually locked me in a room. One day after he left, I found a way to get out and went to my mother's house. Bruce came to my mother's house at 71 Merritt St. and asked to speak with me. I had not shared my concerns with her and so, not knowing, she invited him in.

He took me into my mother's room and I felt something against my head that put me to my knees. He hit me with a gun and split the top of my eyebrow to the white meat. I still have the scar. I got up and he whispered, "I'm taking you back to the room and if you make a scene, I am going to kill your daughter and your mother." So, I walked with him and informed my mother that I was going with Bruce. Until this day, my mother never knew that Bruce hit me and abused me regularly.

When Bruce and I left, he literally dragged me down the stairs. We arrived at Bayside Park and Bruce pistol-whipped me until my face looked like Martin's face when Tommy Hearns beat him up in the ring. I had more lumps on my face and bruises than he did – I could not believe that a man could do that to a woman.

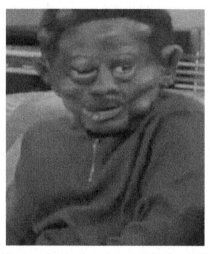

(Scene from the sit-com "Martin")

1 inserted this picture to offer a visual and some comic relief. Although it was a difficult time in my life, I am grateful, through the grace of God, that even though I still can feel the pain, I can reflect and laugh about it now. Thank you, God!

Back to the story. My face was so swollen that I didn't even know who I was. Try to close your eyes

47

and imagine a gun hitting your head. It sounds like your bones are crushing! Every time that gun hit me, I screamed. It was so excruciating. It sounded like a person hitting concrete to break it into little pieces. It was so bad that I did pass out for a moment, and when I came back I felt nothing but PAIN!

He was going to lock me up in the room again, but before that happened, his mother saw me and asked me what happened. I answered her and she told him that if he ever put his hands on me again, she would have him locked up. She asked me if I needed anything, and I said yes (because Bruce told me to say I needed money). She gave it to us, but again, it got ugly. I was too scared to leave and didn't know what else to do.

After that, when he got mad at me, he abused me in other ways. One time, he ripped my clothes off and sodomized me – it was very painful. He said that if I tried to leave again, he would kill me. Well, my dumb ass tried to leave after he made some macaroni and cheese. He did not cook the noodles, but put the sauce on the raw noodles, and then got mad when I wouldn't eat. He got so mad that he ripped my clothes off and sodomized me again. It was extremely painful. He threw me on the floor, grabbed my hair, just started pounding on me, and he inserted his penis into my anus. Again, I am in PAIN! I didn't know what to do then because I was strung out. I couldn't go back home – not the fact that I *could* not, but that I did not want my family to see the condition I was really in.

He said that if I tried to leave again, he would kill me. He beat me up again, but this time I decided that was enough for me. He left to get some drugs and I left to get a bag of dope. As I was getting ready to buy the bag, somebody yelled! "Cathy, RUN! Bruce has his gun out and is looking for you!" So I started running. Because I knew how to get around in the Projects, he couldn't catch me. That was another scary time for me – I saw my life flash before my eyes!

I did not get my dope. My sister had to pick me up and take me to Brooklyn because Bruce had told everybody in the Projects, "You tell Cathy that if I see her, I will kill her!" I was sick when my sister rescued me, but I could not take the chance of risking getting killed. I stayed in Brooklyn until I thought it was safe to return to Jersey City.

This drug and dark age was very devastating. I asked the question, "Why me?! Why is it that I can't get it together?" I don't regret my past because it made me the woman I am today. However, if I had a chance to do it all over again, would I change anything? NO!

*

In this Phase II of my life I had several near-death experiences. I am still pondering what makes a person go from living a normal life to committing incremental suicide. I thought being in the "in-crowd" was the right thing to do, but now I realize when someone tells you to "Keep your friends close, and your enemies closer," I have to say, "Keep your friends closer," because they did more damage to me than my enemies.

Seeing your life flash right in front of you and experiencing the effects of almost being shot, getting pistol whipped down to the white meat, getting sodomized and raped, lets me know that God was watching over me. I cannot express how much pain I felt. I cannot tell you I enjoyed that life.

Let me tell you this - chose your friends wisely and never try drugs because your friends are doing them. They cannot ever explain the side effects when you want to quit!

I can tell you drug withdrawal is brutal. Getting your fix means you can function although you are not functional in a meaningful way. Not one friend told me how to survive in crisis. I tell you today, you will know your friends if you are getting high. Just try stopping and then you'll see who your *real* friends are. Take this from a person who has been there. "Look towards the hills which cometh your help, your help comes from the Lord who made Heaven and Earth." I have seen many things in my life but one thing I never expected was to see myself as a JUNKIE!

At this phase of my life, the hardest thing to do was to stay focused. I thought I had it all figured out and thought I was ready to find another way to live. It happened for a few years, then WOW, here I go again! You never know what path you are going to take. I should have been dead a few times, but I'm still here. Sometimes I sit and tears just run down my cheeks. I am thankful that I am still alive. It did get better for a little while going into Phase III of my life, but again, I started spiraling out of control.

I was then trying to find out, "Who is Cathy?" I have not known her for a long time. I spent my years from 1979-1988, trying to be with the in-crowd, and it almost got me killed. I had a decision to make, and the decision came in 1989. I was working on the Garden State Parkway. Before I start this next phase, I wish to share my daughter's poem.

Tonique's Poem

If I could paint a picture of my life, I'd do it in
blood.
Demons inside of me, sounds of gunshots ring,
but no, I am not no thug,
Just a woman in this world trying to figure out
life and what my purpose is.
Twenty-five, 3 kids ... don't think too much
they know who their father is.
But let's rewind ... take you to the time that
molded the woman I am today,
Three years old, raising my brother, Mommy &
Daddy on drugs anyway.
Wipe your eyes, Nee, it'll be alright.
Naw forget y'all! Y'all know this ain't right!
Memories of my mama nodding, that dope lean.
Visions of monsters ... envy ... yeah, my eyes
were green.
Why me?
Why can't I live carelessly?
Hell, you'd think I was grown, had 2 mouths to
feed,
Seven years old, hey little girl, come walk with
me.

Wise beyond my years, the only thing that kept
me,
"Here baby, here's 50 dollars. Go to the mall ...
you & your brother go crazy."
Confused but numb ... doing this stuff as a
child, but no it wasn't no fun.
Forget it! So, I run.
Took my brother and got the hell out of sight,
Straight to my grandma's house, it's cool here
... it will be alright.
But it wasn't. My mother and father was on that
dumb stuff,
Selfish ways bled on me, like colors mixed with
whites,
Why am I a mother at 10? This isn't even my
fight!
But I did it ....

This is a little insight of what a child at three
years of age to twelve had to endure because of the
decisions I had made as a parent. When I read the
poem, tears run down my cheeks, but I still stand
tall! To God be the glory!

It was a rough time during this phase, but all the
phases have an intriguing emphasis of my life. Here
is a child who took on an adult role at three years
old. I guess you are wondering, "How is it that a
three-year-old little girl is taking care of her
brother?"

Phase III:

Working, Marriage, & Relapse

Well, after I had my son, I relapsed. One day, during another repetitive argument, my little daughter came into the living room and headed toward the door. With a back-pack and her little brother on her hip, she said, "I'm leaving with my little brother because we're tired of hearing you and dad arguing."

We stopped and I looked at my children in dismay, because now here it goes again. I am losing control of my life. Here I am at a point again where I do not want to be alive. Two little children walking out, getting high, about to lose my job, and BAM! The plot thickens.

A memory was rekindled where my oldest daughter had promised that when she turned eighteen, she was returning to get her younger sister and brother. Even though I did take a turn for the better, I had also swirled into a life I never saw coming. So, hold on to your seat, because now I am entering into a life where I am working, making

$21.00 an hour (in the 90's), about to lose my job, and I just do not know how to get this situation under control.

I thought it was bad before, but lo and behold, it got worse! I was working and taking money from the job, but my children's dad was worse. When I said worse, trust me, he had gotten me to the point where I did not care anymore. He took me through hell and back, and here it goes again.

Now, be prepared to understand that in the 90's, making that kind of money and having a pension and a credit union was a big deal! As my daughter said, we were "Balling!" Let me not forget the bonds I had invested in. My daughter, Rahshanan, called it "living the good life!" But it came tumbling down.

Now, 1989, I started working for the Garden State Parkway. I met the father of Tonique and

AlTariq, Greg, while I was working there, through a McDonald's drive-thru window. Thank God all my children were drug free babies! I had Tonique in 1993 and her brother, AlTariq, in 1996. Both pregnancies were bad.

While I was working for the Garden State Parkway, I got robbed at gun-point. Consequently, I had to go on disability and was prescribed anti-depressants, one being Zanex. I took off work for about a month and was collecting worker's compensation. At this point, we were living in Duncan Projects, driving nice cars – a fully loaded Chevrolet Lumina, Hyundai Sonata, and a Hyundai Scoop. All of them, Greg somehow totaled in auto accidents. By the time I had AlTariq, Greg and I had gotten married. Boy, what a turn for the worse.

We found out that his only brother had AIDS. His grandmother had HIV and his grandfather died from HIV. At this point, Greg got ill. The doctors misdiagnosed him with HIV. That is when we found out about his mother and father. Come to find out, he had just taken anti-biotics and had Thrush. This is when his mother told him that she, his brother, and his grandfather had AIDS and HIV. This was devastating for all of us! I can recall vividly when Tonique and Greg's brother, Tony, were in the hospital at the same time. Tonique just had a cold but Tony had been diagnosed with AIDS. Tony was a Yale alumni and very smart. Greg was kind of the "black sheep of the family," like I was, and his mother really showed favoritism toward Tony because she thought he had more going for himself.

The reason why I bring this up is because no child should feel like their mother favors one child over the other. We eventually got married after having Tonique. We regularly fought like enemies. Just when we thought things were getting normal, Tony died. Then his lifelong friend, Angie, died of cancer. Then my father and uncle died. These were trying and emotionally draining times. I started taking/overdosing prescription medication to numb the pain and function – substituting these for street drugs.

After I had my son, AlTariq, in 1996, I didn't know I was pregnant again. I went to work and one of the supervisors and I got into an argument and I had a heart attack. I was taken out of work on a stretcher. When I got to the hospital, they gave me nitroglycerin and my blood pressure was extremely high. I stayed in the hospital for four days. When I got out, I didn't feel normal – something was wrong with my body. I disregarded the pain and continued to work, pulling heavy vaults, carrying heavy money bags, and taking my pills. So, I went for a checkup because I had missed my period. Come to find out, I was four months pregnant. At this time, I didn't want to be with Greg anymore because I was having a difficult pregnancy, we kept fighting, and I was emotionally and mentally drained from all the family health issues, work, and marriage.

I considered abortion and was talking with my sister, Pat, about how I felt. She said, "Girl, oh no you are not, that could be your boy!" So, I reconsidered and didn't abort. It turned out to be one of the worst pregnancies ever. I never saw Greg – he seldom came by because he was out drinking. When he did come by, we would start fighting. One time, after he left, I found his wallet and took the money out. I told my daughter, Rahshanan, to mail it to Jersey City where I would later retrieve it. During my crisis, Angie and Abdul would come and sit with me every night because Greg was never home. They would leave when I was about to go to sleep. In the morning, when I got up, Tonique (at three years old) would have to move my legs because I was in so much pain from being pregnant with AlTariq. What kind of man was this who had no concerns for his unborn child? He didn't even take care of his own children, Zakyrr and Ahmyrr. I should have heeded the signs. Then, to top it all off, he had the nerve to treat me like dirt!

It wasn't all that bad in East Orange. I was gainfully employed for several years. My daughter, Rahshanan, had come back to stay with us. She remembers good meals like turkey wings and stuffing, oxtails, pistachio cake, and macaroni and cheese. Those were good times! Rahshanan said that those were some of her best memories! Rahshanan moved back to my mother's house and I had AlTariq thereafter. I went back to work, lost a little weight, and was on a good roll!

I returned to work and they sent me to Irvington North plaza. A man, a vault supervisor, would pass through my lane and would roll his eyes and never speak – like a dog. He had to come and check the vaults at Irvington North and ended up in my booth. We had a conversation and I was puzzled because he had never spoken to me before. I had heard rumors that he was sleeping around with most of the women on the Parkway. I was collecting tolls and put my hand out of the window to collect the toll when I heard someone say, "Cathy." I turned around and he had his dick out of his pants. I was shocked and told him if he didn't put his dick back in his pants, he's going to have a serious problem with me.

I was traumatized. I called the supervisor and asked if I could shut down my lane. I went into the corner and started crying. The flashbacks of the men who had abused me in the past surfaced, and it was unbearable. I cried for about a half hour, got myself together, went back to the plaza, and was met by the nicest man I've ever met, named Tony. He saw the tears in my eyes and asked what was wrong. I just broke down crying. I told him what had happened at the Irvington North plaza and he asked, "Was it that damn Franklin?"

I said, "Yes, it was." He told me to go report it now. I told the supervisor and they told me I could leave early. I hadn't returned since then.

I started taking pills again and what they didn't know, after I had AlTariq, Greg was back around.

59

Because of how I was treated by him when I was pregnant, I convinced myself that the only time I was happy was when I was high. Sad but true. One day, I said to Greg, "You know what? I want to get high. Go find me some cocaine." That M-F'er went and got it: baking soda, stem, lighter, and drugs. Who would've thought that your own husband would appease that request? But come to find out, he was already getting high again.

The world became dark and gloomy. I could not find my way out. I saw that I just wanted to feel good and let all my pain go away. It is not possible, it is not fair, but this is real-life stuff that happens every day. I tried turning to the right, but the dope man was there; I tried turning to the left, but the cocaine man was there.

I turn straight, and the methadone center was telling me to come on in, but NO! I liked getting high. I liked the bull-crap I was doing. I got a thrill knowing I could get any man I wanted! My walk told a man that if you act right and have the right money, you can get the cookie. The women hated me and the men loved me. It did not matter because I wanted what I wanted and knew I could get it!

What was my name? I had many names when I was tricking – you do not have just one name, you have several. I might be Gloria one week and Cynthia the next, but only Cathy when I was home. Call me what you deem too, but please put a Ms. on it. I was sexy, had the walk, the talk, and what all the men wanted. You ask, "What was that?" It was whatever they desired, they received.

My journey was very difficult and challenging for me: getting locked up, going to rehab, boosting, tricking, selling, buying, getting clean, relocating, college, counselor, and finally getting ordained as a minister and evangelist. Many situations occurred during this time and I wanted to start this phase off with my daughter's perspective, because it was also very difficult for her to raise her brother at such a young age.

My son AlTariq does not remember those days when his parents were using drugs. How do I know? I asked him if he wanted to write his story of growing up with both parents being addicts, AlTariq responded that he did not remember those times because Tonique guarded him from whatever she could. "However," he said, "I do remember you and dad using drugs." (He had a confused face.) I asked him if that was all he remembered and he responded with, "Yes!" Thanks to Nene (that is what AlTariq called Tonique, because he could not pronounce her name). Tonique did an excellent job protecting and shielding her brother from the MADNESS that they had to endure.

Tonique/AlTariq's Story

Where do I begin? As long as I can remember, my life had been hard. From being a "mother" for my brother to exposure to drugs and weird people, as you can imagine, my life was not for the faint-of-heart. I remember living with my mom and dad around the age of 3 or 4. That was back when we lived in East Orange, New Jersey. It was a very dirty and scary place. I would go outside often with my little brother in tow. I made it my duty to protect him from this cruel world we were living in. Though I didn't understand why we had to deal with this lifestyle, I would always wipe those tears and keep it in as I pushed into another day. East Orange was a bad time. I remember my mom and dad getting into a fight. I nearly lost my life that day. One-minute, I am out in the hallway of our apartment, and the next thing I know I'm dodging a knife that's being thrown across the hall. Traumatizing, right? Yeah, it's a lot for some adults to handle. Imagine suffering from that as a young child. Whenever my parents got too far gone with the drugs, they would send us to live with a relative. I've always admired my mother for that. Despite her addiction, she always saw to it that we were under great care whenever things got too bad. She always was a mother first. I reflect back and compare my past life to others who may have had similar backgrounds. I always feel a warm sensation, a feeling that felt like confirmation that one day my parents would snap out of it. My mother could have let her addiction take over. What if I got sold for drugs? I heard horror stories of mothers selling off their children in exchange for drugs and money and it made me sick. I am forever thankful that at least my mother never lost her morals and love for her children during her battle.

Life with my Aunt Poochie and grandmother was refreshing, to say the least. I felt secure; my brother and I finally had a feel of stability. Things were really beginning to look up. We started to live the life of normal little children, though I still had nightmares and thoughts about what we went through. Fast forward to me being in 5th grade. We were back with our parents at this point and it seemed like things had gotten a bit worse. We were living with different people, in basements. The basement was just something I could not handle anymore. We had to "go to the bathroom" in a hole in the floor of the bathroom. The lady whose basement we stayed in had so many roaches and was filthy. I remember vividly getting handed $100 and being told by my dad to take my brother to the mall and have fun. Yes, at 10 years old, I was taking myself and my then 7-year-old brother to the mall. We would ride the Newport Local on the NJ transit all the way to Newport Mall. I recall us walking around aimlessly, spending money on childish things, all to escape our messed-up reality. One day when we were leaving the mall, we got on the wrong bus. I guess I had not paid attention to my surroundings. I was a kid. We got off on the first exit when I realized that we were going in the wrong direction. Once off the bus, I noticed an odd guy down the road, standing with what looked like a chainsaw in his hand. I was terrified, but one thing in the life I lived, I was always prepared to run and not fall for traps. No sooner than that feeling came, the guy started running towards us. I grabbed my brother and we ran as fast as we could. God sent a few angels that night because when we hit Montgomery projects, there were 3 women outside who saw us running. They knew we were afraid. It was a gamble, but I trusted them to get us home to our parents safely. They did. At this point, my mother knew it was time to send us away again. We moved in with my older sister, Rahshanan.

Zombie Land

My daughter talked about the part she played in her brother's life and what she had to endure. I have to tell you how this all went from good to bad. After I relapsed, it just got worse, and to say that it was bad would be an understatement. Here I go again getting high – free-basing, heroine, and now crack is introduced into my world. It was horrible. The children had to go many times to stay with my mother, sister, daughter, and even one time with a friend of mine, but I wanted them safe.

I would like to fast forward a little bit and again have you close your eyes to picture my life. I moved from East Orange, Jersey City, then to Bronx, New York. These were places I would not wish on my worst enemy. East Orange was a place where I lived on Williams and Walnut, and I was surrounded by drug dealers, addicts, junkies, prostitutes, and johns, but no children. The women would dress accordingly and some even more provocative as shown in the picture below.

I was staying in a boarding house were everybody got high. It was total nightmare, to say the least. I got deeper into drugs, prostituting, and even became a Madam for the little hookers who were out there, dirty, and didn't have anywhere to stay. The deal was that on the third, I would buy them clothes, make them look descent, and then they would hustle for drugs and food. They did not like Greg. They thought he was greedy and a butthole. It was scary and we all walked around like zombies.

I thought my situation would get better, so I called my mother and asked her if we could move in with her. For a while, it worked. However, my habit got worse and worse and she threw Greg and me out. We started staying in an abandoned building again, because in East Orange, I did not want to pay rent and wind up homeless and having to stay up all night so we wouldn't get robbed.

Then, we began living on Bidwell Ave. in Jersey City with this addict that Greg had met. Well, the lights were off and there was garbage when you entered into the house. On the second floor, where Greg and I were staying, the tub had feces in it and the smell was horrendous, but still I stayed so I could get high. The stench was so bad that my own brother told me to come home. But hey, I did not care. I just wanted to get high.

The Bronx was an experience I will never ever forget, but I am thankful for that experience because this is part of my testimony that, "God is a miracle worker." I moved to the Bronx and when I got there, I was sick and did not have any money for methadone, heroine, or pills. I was so sick that I could not get out the bed. See, Greg informed me that he had a methadone clinic I could go to so he could use the last bit of money we had to buy crack. Of course, I went along with him.

We smoked the last bit of crack and Greg, my children, and I were on our way to the Bronx. Just as we were leaving, my buddy, "ride or die" cousin Harold, came by and said, "Hey! I'm taking you all to the Bronx." I will never forget that day because it was September 1, 2001 – the World Trade Center attack. You see, God was in the mist of this too, because if it were not for my cousin driving us to the Bronx, we would not be here. We would have been in the World Trade Center. God's grace and mercy saved us even when we did not know it.

Gleason Avenue in the Bronx was where I really spiraled out of control. I was selling drugs, getting locked up, boosting, getting people hurt, and didn't know who I was. I was like a zombie. We stayed in the Bronx for three or four years and I promise you, I think I got a week of sleep. I got high EVERY DAY until the time I moved back to Jersey City with my mother again. Looking like a zombie was a scary thing, but I did not care.

"Travesty" is a good word to express how I lived in the Bronx. I met people who I never thought I would ever be entertained by with their manipulations. I walked into a world of boosting, drug dealing, incarceration, and street-walking.

Not only was I involved in all the other bull, I started messing with counterfeit money. I would wait for Greg to return home from work because he had a connection that would give us $500.00 of fake money for $100.00. I would leave New York at 2:00 in the morning, travel to New Jersey to purchase drugs from the drug dealers (hoping I wouldn't get caught with the counterfeit money), and catch the train back home.

It worked for a while until one day, early in the morning around 3:00 am, I traveled again to purchase drugs with my friend and we coped the drugs. Everything was good until we had to go back out that same morning. We went to the same dealers and they caught us. We were in the car with a detective (who got high) and we could not say anything because they would have killed us all. So, they pulled up to the car and said, "Give me my drugs and my money you passed from this fake $100.00 bill!"

We tried to convince them we were not the ones, but they, of course, remembered my friend. They put a gun through the window and we handed over what we had left. They told us to never come back. That was very scary for me and when we drove off the detective said, "I'm glad we survived this, but don't worry, I will get them." You know what he did? Come to find out, he would rob drug dealers. He made sure he told me, "I got them back for you, baby." He also was one of my men who I hung with. I found myself fighting, surviving in Rikers Island, and avoiding getting caught up in a murder conspiracy.

This world turned me into a MONSTER! I met this young lady named Lady V; she was a booster and she was how I got involved in the world of boosting (stealing). When she first introduced me to this lifestyle, I was really scared, but then when I started learning the skill, it was like a rush. I mean, I actually got off knowing that I had just gotten away with over a thousand dollars' worth of clothes from places like Macy's, K-Mart, Marshall's, Old Navy, etc. Wherever I could steal from, I did. It was amazing to go into a store dressed up like a nurse, a nun, a pregnant woman, a man, even a child, and get away with it. I thought it was cool.

However, when I started getting locked up, it still did not stop me. I can remember the first time I got locked up for stealing. The security guard and I fought. He was about 6'5" and 350 lbs. He hit me and I almost fell. When I got up, I almost knocked him down. We fought for about five minutes and I said to him, "Is that all you got?" He got mad and called the cops. At this time, I was informed by the cops that I should press charges because, in order to get charged for stealing, I had to have left the store.

After getting locked up for boosting, it seemed like I kept getting locked up. The next time was for a couple of bags of heroine. Then it got worse and I had to do a program to avoid getting six months in jail. It did not stop there. My house got raided and again I got locked up. My husband turned on me and told them to charge me with the drug charges. I did do time for that.

It just got worse and worse, but the time that really bothered me the most was when "Sticky Fingers" was shot and killed. (Sticky Fingers was the big time drug dealer who I used to push drugs for.) When I came home, I was informed that they had shot and killed Sticky Fingers and his woman, Lady M. It was sad because I could have saved his life. I used to push drugs from drug dealers around the corner as well, so I was in the middle. Because I was locked up, they set-up Sticky Fingers.

I stayed high day in and day out. The years of being a zombie are the years that so many things happened to me. So, I decided again to give my children to my sister, Liz, to take care of them.

I was in jail, out of jail, in jail, and out of jail so much that I did not want to leave. Hell, I had three square meals, methadone, and no children. When I finally had to leave, I told the Sargent that I wanted to stay and she said, "You do not have to go home, but you have to leave here."

I cried, "I don't want to go! Everything I need is here!" But I got released and went back to the same thing.

My life in the Bronx was a nightmare, but I survived and it is sad when I see teenagers today on drugs because they have no idea what road they are going down. There is a dispensation of technology – take advantage of it and be the best you can be. I would never introduce anybody to drugs, boosting, prostituting, or how to make fast money. What I learned is that fast money goes fast. Some might get lucky and survive if they sell drugs, but what is the sense of having the money and have to look over your back all the time for the cops, stick-up men, snitches, and enemies?

After moving from the Bronx back to Jersey City, I was so skinny that my sister Liz got scared. I could see the hurt in her eyes. I would call my mother to make sure she informed Liz that I was alright, but this last time coming back from the Bronx, I almost broke her. I decided I would not give up until I beat this habit which I call "JUNKIE!"

I have been to many Rehab Facilities and every time I got out, I would get a bag of dope and would go inside to cook up some cocaine and ride the train and bus getting high with my children's dad. I have been to over twenty rehab facilities, but I was not going to stop until I was a winner. It took a while, but I was not giving up. I took people's money, I scammed people, I tricked with men, and I did what I had to do to survive.

Fast forward … I finally got sick Christmas day, 2004. I was staying in the basement of a Pastor and she informed us we had to leave because she was going out and she did not trust my husband and me at the time. Before I got out of the bed, I remembered something that my mother had said that stuck with me. That was, "When you get to a place and you can't call on anybody else, call on Jesus." I was so sick that day that I said a prayer, "Lord, please help me and put me in the hospital January fourth and I will forever serve You and do the best I can to know You." Thank you, Mom; that prayer worked.

When I woke up that Christmas I was so sick that I could barely walk. My children's dad helped me walk to my daughter's house and when I tell you I felt like pure HELL, I cannot describe how bad it was. I felt horrible, but I made it there. My son-in-law gave me money to buy a bag of heroine because he understood my pain. My daughter had tears in her eyes and my son-in-law was so caring that day. I cannot express how thankful I was for that money. I pray that nobody would ever have to experience that pain. However, there is always one who gets hooked on that thing we call "DRUGS." I still can see my daughter's face and it brings tears to my eyes still today.

I know there are a lot of things I have to work out with her, but I know God is in control and one day I will have the best relationship with my daughter. She deserves that and more. All of my children deserve to see their mother be a mother.

Phase IV:

Relocate to Georgia

I decided to move to Georgia after I returned home from rehab at Rye Hospital in New York City. After I left the hospital, I went to my sister's house to stay clean until I left for Georgia. I arrived at my sister Liz's house at night, around 9:00 pm. I had my two grandsons with me because I knew I would be leaving soon for Georgia to live with my sister.

Everything was going fine. I started to go upstairs and the doorbell rang. I went to answer the door and something told me to keep going up the stairs, even though I was right by the door. I shouted for Liz to get the door. She replied, "Why don't *you* get the door?" I started laughing and kept walking. Liz answered the door and it was the cops. My sister asked them why were they at her door and they informed her that they were looking for Catherine Bailey.

I heard that and my heart started beating really fast. I tip-toed and hid under the bed. I whispered in my sister Pat's ear, "Please go downstairs and pretend it was you who came up the stairs."

The cops asked my sister, "Well, is Catherine Bailey here?" Of course, my sister Liz informed them that I was not there. They asked her who was that who went upstairs – they had seen her through the door. Immediately my sister answered and said that it was my other sister, Pat.

The cop asked if they could speak to her, so Liz called Pat and said to her, "I told the cops it was you upstairs and they don't believe me."

Pat said, "I will be down when I finish wrapping my hair." Now in the meantime, I am scared to death and sill hiding under the bed. Pat went downstairs and said in front of the officers, "What is the problem?"

Liz responded, "The cops think that you are Cathy."

Pat said, "Do I need to show my identification to you? Did you not hear my sister inform you that I was not Cathy and she is not here?" They looked at Pat's identification and said, "Goodnight."

My sister Pat is very dear to me. She has been there for me through thick and thin. She has always been good to me even when I was on drugs. Now understand, we have had our ups and our downs, but our ups are better than our downs. She has been there for me since I had moved and I cannot ask for a better sister. The cops left and my sister called my sister, Beatty, to ask if I could come around her house when the cops leave and she said, "No! Greg does not want her around here." That hurt my heart and my sister was hurt too. After the cops left, Liz took me to my sister Geneva's house.

It was a very scary night for me and I just really wanted to get out of Jersey City and move on with my life. I arrived at my sister's house and she let me stay until the next morning. Around 7:00 am, I hear "Get the f... out now! You better get up because when I leave, you and Greg are leaving too!" I woke up sick as a dog and could barely walk. I was so weak that Greg had to literally carry me out through the snow on the ground. It was cold as all get out! I felt like I was living at the North Pole.

Crying, I called my sister because I had nowhere to go. She told me she would call my niece, Trina, and she did. Through the grace and mercy of God, Greg and I made it to her house. I got in bed, still sick, so Greg went and brought me a bag of heroine to make me feel better. I stayed there for a week and then, Liz and my mother on the third of February, rushed Greg and me to the Greyhound Bus Station. I was on my way to Georgia.

Now, before I left, I went and got four bags of dope and sniffed them on the way down. By the time I got to Georgia, I had one bag left. When I finally arrived in Georgia, I thought everything was going to be just great.

A New Life

We arrived in Georgia February 4, 2005, and as soon as I stepped off the bus, I heard a voice say to me, "Gregory Bailey is going to do to you everything he thought you did to him and more."

I did not understand then, but I understand now Who was speaking to me. I turned to Greg and said, "Greg, if you think that you do not want to be with me and you think you cannot forgive for what you think I did, you can go to your friend Jackie's house and I can go with my sister."

Greg responded, "No, I want to be where you are."

Now, I know what I heard. We were now at my sister's house. We left our children with my sister, Liz, until we could get an apartment and Greg could get a job. I was on Social Security Disability. After four days there, I got withdrawals and now I am really sick again: bad headache, nausea, can't eat, and can't get out of bed. My sister looked in the room because she had not seen me all day and saw I was sick and said, "Go to the hospital. You don't look good at all."

I barely could lift my head so Greg helped me out of the bed. My sister informed us that we should go to Grady's Hospital. When we got there, I informed the nurse what the problem was. She took my blood pressure and it was 315/265. I was lying on the bed and couldn't move because I was in so much pain. I heard them say, "Code Blue!" They rushed me into the back and put something under my tongue. Later on I found out it was nitro-glycerin so to avoid a heart attack and to bring my blood pressure down.

The nurse asked me what was wrong and with a soft voice and my head pounding, I told her that I was going through withdrawals from heroine. She asked if I needed methadone. I quickly responded and said slowly, "No, I need to suffer like Jesus in order to beat this monster. (I could never take the suffering Jesus did but it was telling me, "God's got you!"). I stayed at the hospital all night and left so my sister Felicia could go to work. I saw the tears in her eyes and just whispered to her because I was too sick to talk much, "God's got me!"

Before she left she said, "Cathy, read the Bible." I said alright, but when I started to read, I would get sleepy and I would put it down. She would call and ask, "Did you read the Bible?" I told her that I tried but I don't understand what I'm reading and I keep falling asleep. Felicia said, "Cathy, why don't you start with Ezekiel?" I started and kept praying. As soon as I was able to get out of bed, I started to read the Bible all day.

After I was doing better, Greg started looking for a job. It was a month after we had arrived in Georgia because he waited until I was stable enough to be home by myself. He was blessed enough by God's grace and mercy to get a job interview at Wal-Mart.

I was reading my Bible and I heard Greg ask, "Do you want to go with me to this interview?"

I responded with, "No." Then something said, "Go." (Again I am baffled because I am hearing a voice that sounds like me but I know it is *not* me.) So I said, "Yes, I want to go." Then the voice said for me to bring my Bible. (It was starting to get scary because I heard this voice so clearly.) Lo and behold, I went, and as we were waiting for them to call Greg (I was still reading my Bible), I heard this woman's voice and she said, "Gregory Bailey." Again the voice said for me to look up! I looked up and the voice said to me, "This is the woman who will take your husband."

Okay! What was happening to me? I was hearing this voice so clearly and everything it was saying to me was unusual – I didn't know what was going on with me. Well, an hour passed and Greg finally came out. I looked at him and that voice said, "Tell him what I told you."

I knew Greg would think I was crazy, but I told him anyway and he said, "You did not hear that." To make a long story short, after eighteen years of marriage, the voice that told me that this woman was going to take my husband was right – it happened two years later. Greg divorced me and married her a month after. After going through several hospitals for my blood pressure, getting locked up, getting put in a Mental Hospital, almost going crazy, and trying to take my life, I finally realized that God was with me all the time. As I sit here and write this book, I realize those voices I was hearing were from the Spirit of God getting me prepared for what I was going to go through.

It was a hard road for me in Georgia. I did not believe that a little woman like me would go through all that I went through and survive. I do realize that God's grace and mercy have been with me all this time. Even though I went through so much, I am still here. My sister Liz had to help me out with my children because I did not understand how to raise them after being a junkie for over twenty years. I do realize that all my trials, tribulations, and storms are now my blessings. I understand that God is a way-maker, miracle worker, promise keeper, light in the darkness, a doctor in the hospital, a teacher in the classroom, my counselor in the middle of the night, my friend when nobody else was there, my heart regulator, my rock, my shepherd, and my hero!

Even though I went through all that I went through, God allowed me to go to a Seminary and I receive my Bachelor's Degree in Counseling, my Master's Degree in Counseling, and five classes short from my second Master's Degree in Divinity. I am also an Ordained Minister/Evangelist. God knew I would need a Church to teach me Christian Ministry, so I was sent to Solid Ground Christian Ministries. My Bishop is James Wilson. He and

First Lady Wilson have been good to me and my family. I could not have asked God for a better Church.

Now, do not misunderstand, it has been a rocky road for me at Solid Ground, but it was something God wanted me to learn. However, Bishop and First Lady have the best heart and they really love me as much as I love them. Believe me, we have had our shouting matches, our disagreements, and disrespect, but through it all, God allows me to be the Woman of God I am today. Bishop James Wilson is the one God used to ordain me as Minister/Evangelist. It was a hard journey, but it made me grow.

I have to mention my Spiritual Mother, Pastor Churn. With everything I went through, she was always there for me. It did not matter what it was my Spirit would lead me to call her about, but whenever she said, "Thus sayest the Lord," it came to pass. Pastor Churn has been with me for over twelve years, and still today she is with me. This is not because of me, but because when you take things out of *your* hands and put them in *God's* hands, God will make it happen. That is what God will do for you. God will also send somebody to help you on this journey.

My story is not over with because God is not finished with me yet! I am still being tested, I am still being transformed, and I am still holding on to God's unchanging hand. I have chosen to have Supreme Love for God and I chose to do what God has called me to do. That is be a good sheep and lean not on my own understanding. Trust in God and God will order your steps.

My song is not over, my mission is not completed, my pain is getting better, the thorn is still in my side, but I know, yes, I know that God is in CONTROL!

Cave after cave after cave and as the old adage says, "What does not kill you will make you stronger." But what God is saying is, "Cast your

burdens unto me and I shall give you rest!" Walk by *faith* and not by *sight*! I am thankful to be alive and I do appreciate that God saw something in me to save me. I came to Georgia looking a hot mess, but through God's transformation, I am starting to look normal as you can see.

Getting ordained as a Minister/Evangelist was God's plan for me. As I mentioned earlier, my story is not over. I am God's Ambassador:

Let us bow our heads, "O Heavenly Father, I come to You as humbly as I know how. I confess my sins, those known and unknown. Lord, You know I am not perfect and fall short every day of my life. I want to take time out to say, 'Thank You for Your grace and mercy. Thank You for our life, our health, our strength, my family, my friends, the roof over our heads, food on our table, the shoes on our feet, the clothes on our backs, my transportation, and everything I know You have provided for us. And thank You for seeing us through danger, seen and unseen.' Amen!"